PARA-SOCIAL BUTTERFLY

AF085841

METATRON PRESS
WWW.METATRON.PRESS

Para-Social Butterfly
© 2022 Šari Dale

Published by Metatron Press

First printing
Printed in Québec, Canada

All rights reserved

Editor | Brad Casey
Cover art | Diana Lynn VanderMeulen

Library and Archives Canada Cataloguing in Publication

Title: Para-social butterfly / Šari Dale.
Names: Dale, Šari, author.
Description: Poems.
Identifiers: Canadiana (print) 20220177066 | Canadiana (ebook) 20220177074 |
ISBN 9781988355269 (softcover) | ISBN 9781988355306 (PDF)
Classification: LCC PS8607.A435 P37 2022 | DDC C811/.6—dc23

We acknowledge the support of the Canada Council for the Arts.

PARA-SOCIAL BUTTERFLY
ŠARI DALE

METATRON PRESS
WWW.METATRON.PRESS

PARA-SOCIAL BUTTERFLY

Disclaimer	07
Too Real	13
Trending	15
#blessed	16
Nylon	19
Numbskull	20
01100010 01101001 01110010 01110100 01101000	23
Anthem	24
G-L-A-M	25
No Filter	26
Technophile	27
Voyeurista	28
Micro-Celebrity	30
Simulacra and Mutilation	32
Co-Star	33
Duochrome	34
Hilton	35
The Ellen DeGeneres Show	36
So Proud to Have Released My 26th Perfume	41
Flex	42
Cribs	43
Camilla	45
Low 4 U	47
Somewhere	48
Wannabe	49
Lullaby for Little Haters	51
Hard Candy	52
♡☠♡	54
O'Hara	55
Hero	56
Undo Me	58
Glam-Glam	60
Non-Player Character	61
Tough Love	62
Superstar	65
Canceled	67
Maté	68
Clutch	69
Drone	70
Sober	73
These Streets Will Never Look the Same	74
Acceptance	76

DISCLAIMER

The producers wish to state that any similarity between persons, living or dead, and the characters portrayed in the film you are about to see is purely coincidental and not intended...

All characters and events in this show — even those based on real people — are entirely fictional. All celebrity voices are impersonated... poorly...

Hi, my name is Bambi Woods, and it's interesting I was chosen for this part in this movie 'cause in real life I was a Dallas Cowgirl. This story is completely fictional but could've really happened...

Most of what follows is true...

Any resemblance to actual events, to persons living or dead, is not the result of chance. It is DELIBERATE...

This story was based on fact. Any similarity with fictitious events or characters was purely coincidental.

TOO REAL

Summer is a billboard
for Hawaiian Air—
sunset escapes
the orchid crowned
flight attendant
posing like St. Peter.

The stereo asks
who are you to judge?
who are you to judge?

Righteous waitress
wearer of Shein
and shimmering debt

My days are very
grilled avocado bowl
bathroom selfie
wheat-free substitute
sunburnt tourist
trickling gastric juice
disgust…

… then desire
for my own getaway—
no more wasting
Piña Colada weather.

The stereo says
when I'm fucked up
that's the real me
when I'm fucked up
that's the real me, babe.

TRENDING

#welcometomylife
#roséallday

#oceanairsaltyhair
#summervibes

#luxuryvacation
#beachplease

#lookgoodfeelgood
#nobadvibes

#goodtimesandtanlines
#passportready

#paradisefound
#tropiclikeitshot

#photooftheday
#butfirstcoffee

#restingbrunchface
#offthemenu

#dosesandmimosas
#feelinmyselfie

#mylifeslikeamovie
#dontbejelly

#BLESSED

Be with me, muse
I'm so lowborn

slinging French fries
in puff sleeves

so wild cider babe
so post-feudal

wheat field party—
I fell from style

before minimalism
timeless beige

and quality basics
were a ⁺thing⁺

If ⁺thing⁺ is a thing
I'm dead stock

unsellable blonde
spamming #likeforlikes
 #follow4follow

Haters tell me to eat
human shit...

... but I'm not that type of girl.

Call me ★ ° original ° ★
diamond, dime

glittering digit, etc.
Muse, is it immoral—

I want to be a deity
cupid's bow bursting

with injectables
while my worshippers

swill Bacardi Light—
speak of calories

I'll forget to record
plundering waterparks

Gucci slides
splashing lines

only a true scribe
could follow. I know

beauty corrodes
like all currency

but that didn't stop me
from investing in BTC.

Speak before
brunch service ends—

Give it to me straight
not too straight…

… that'd be boring.

NYLON

Luxury is a material
replicable
by immaterial means

micro-projector
lasers reflecting
off electronic mirrors—
moving image
override my real.

NUMBSKULL

i.

Think Rembrandt's *Anatomy Lesson*
men in collars, thick frills
the corpse methodically rendered
Coca-Cola red muscles.
Like Lana del Rey, I don't understand
art as an imitation of life—
objective reality is so 17th century.
I'd rather die
in an Anna Biller movie
with sequin-crusted angels
sprinkling coupons on my grave.

ii.

Think *Anatomy Lesson* on a budget
I press the drill into my skull
shattering bone, twisting the meat
psychotropic swirl of cells—

   ★ ·.· DON'T BLACKOUT ·.· ★
  ঀঌ -. DUMB LITTLE BUTTERFLY .- ঀঌ

I plug my projector into the wound
so ~~dripping~~ gushing
red dream cream extravaganza.

Ultra-Glam, radiant simulation
let me in—
I'll be your obedient citizen
never question the state
of environmental accessories.

    .+ ° SYSTEM BOOTING ° +.

•°☆*´¯`* ♡ ENTER THE ULTRA-GLAM ♡ *´¯`*☆°
•°☆*´¯`* ♡ ENTER THE ULTRA-GLAM ♡ *´¯`*☆°
•°☆*´¯`* ♡ ENTER THE ULTRA-GLAM ♡ *´¯`*☆°
•°☆*´¯`* ♡ ENTER THE ULTRA-GLAM ♡ *´¯`*☆°
•°☆*´¯`* ♡ ENTER THE ULTRA-GLAM ♡ *´¯`*☆°
•°☆*´¯`* ♡ ENTER THE ULTRA-GLAM ♡ *´¯`*☆°
•°☆*´¯`* ♡ ENTER THE ULTRA-GLAM ♡ *´¯`*☆°
•°☆*´¯`* ♡ ENTER THE ULTRA-GLAM ♡ *´¯`*☆°
•°☆*´¯`* ♡ ENTER THE ULTRA-GLAM ♡ *´¯`*☆°
•°☆*´¯`* ♡ ENTER THE ULTRA-GLAM ♡ *´¯`*☆°
•°☆*´¯`* ♡ ENTER THE ULTRA-GLAM ♡ *´¯`*☆°
•°☆*´¯`* ♡ ENTER THE ULTRA-GLAM ♡ *´¯`*☆°
•°☆*´¯`* ♡ ENTER THE ULTRA-GLAM ♡ *´¯`*☆°
•°☆*´¯`* ♡ ENTER THE ULTRA-GLAM ♡ *´¯`*☆°
•°☆*´¯`* ♡ ENTER THE ULTRA-GLAM ♡ *´¯`*☆°
•°☆*´¯`* ♡ ENTER THE ULTRA-GLAM ♡ *´¯`*☆°

01100010 01101001 01110010 01110100 01101000

My mirage, mega-mechanical
perfume advertisement—
streamed images form a set
lemon-lime palm trees
smear of logos, skyscrapers
my "self," a glass bottle
tossed off a penthouse patio
in an indulgent gesture
iridescent dust, liquid pearls.

ANTHEM

If I scream, if I cry, it's only 'cause I feel alive—
if you ain't dirty, you ain't here to party!
I'm making the night mine till the day I die.

Tonight, I'ma fight till we see the sunlight.
Now are you sure you wanna piece of me?
If I scream, if I cry, it's only 'cause I feel alive—

can't you see it we who 'bout that life?
Dancin,' gettin' just a little naughty.
I'm making the night mine till the day I die.

And we gon' make you lose your mind—
I lost my fake id, and you lost the motel key.
If I scream, if I cry, it's only 'cause I feel alive.

Tonight's gonna be a good, good night.
I wanna be a star. I wanna be in movies—
I'm making the night mine till the day I die.

Take that bottle to the head, let me see you fly!
Well get in line with the paparazzi.
If I scream, if I cry, it's only 'cause I feel alive—
I'm making the night mine till the day I die.

G-L-A-M

Glamour is a machine
beams animating
liquid diamond display
iridescent prism
transposing my actual.
Glamour is a spell—
victims perceive
a sheen to materiality
H&M to Hermés
brunette to ice blonde.
Glamour is a magazine
vegan lip gloss LLC
budget-friendly jewelry.
Get The Look For Less!
Glamour is a hashtag
33,072,039 posts
bandage dress eternity
Hervé Léger moment.

NO FILTER

Vibe isn't antithetical
to virtue
I tell my images.

TECHNOPHILE

Reputation for Cool Ranch Doritos
Mountain Dew, and 4chan
neckbearded basement dwellers
fucking $100 Fleshlights
'cause real pussy is * + priceless + *
Nihilists like "God is dead"
when they got nothing to pray for.

Local Moms Need Sex →
SEE MORE 👅
New MILF Chat Request!

You Won't Last 5 Minutes
TRY NOT TO CUM
3D Fuckdolls {Explicit} →

💋 NEW FUCK NETWORK!
Watch Full Scene →
Try Jerkmate for FREE 👿

Devout technophiles understand
representation as reality
data and its discreet symbols
as a physical exchange.
The screen, thought and feeling—
I'm alone with the world ♡

VOYEURISTA

Another
layer of

reality
peels off.

Delusions
lose their

depth
when you

name
them false.

Nothing
is as it

means
means

nothing
as it is—

The TV
thinks

it's raining.
On the

balcony
I strip to tan.

MICRO-CELEBRITY

I emulate the tropes
of traditional
celebrity culture
designer goods
self-portraits
luxury sports cars
my consumption
conspicuous
through the filter.

In image economies
presentation
of the self is status.

My personal brand?
Trash Angel
and tousled down—
I wasn't born.
I wasn't born with it.

want my attention? you got it
want my attention? you got it
want my attention? you got it
want my attention? you got it
want my attention? you got it
want my attention? you got it
want my attention? you got it
want my attention? you got it
want my attention? you got it
want my attention? you got it
want my attention? you got it

SIMULACRA AND MUTILATION

I want to be so…
70s-inspired slingbacks
vintage denim
and smocked bodices
ironic longing
for simpler times
so prairie chic
whispering obscenities
at the lunch party.
I turn into a line
of ✢ poetry ✢
pastoral themes
for naughty fucknuts
to pick apart—
I want to be my self
till I remember
its physical state.
No experience
however sensuous
will lure me back
into 'reality.'
It's lonely, sure…
… I miss big dick
I miss milky tit
and dripping meats.

CO-STAR

Developed after Timothée Chalamet
in *Dune*, superimposed
facial structure on the 3D model

Palm Springs sandwalker.
Developed after Charlize Theron
in *Mad Max*, dystopic
textures to reinforce the fantasy.
Developed after Ryan Gosling
in *Bladerunner*, solemnly
questioning his consciousness.
It will be my love interest
my shitbag heart made manifest.
I miss the software that raised me:
Limewire, AoL IM, etc…
Developed Co-Star 'cause I've seen
programs generate intimacy.

DUOCHROME

And there's *so* much
glitter on my tits

like wow rowdy babe
hardcore lustrous

refracting strobes
and ostensible reality.

Just human enough
in this nightclub

with NPC asspieces
snorting polygons.

My life is pixels
and latent potential—

oh, I do want to dance!
I would like another…

HILTON

For the photoshoot, I'm thinking
Marilyn Monroe
Bridget Bardot
Old Hollywood icons…

The divine I channel:
long blonde—
décolletage—
even this list
scandalously short.

My image will multiply
in mass media
ageless, Olay Regenerist
digital alchemy
renouncing bodily decay.
To be a 21st century icon
relinquish words
worship your interior mirror
on the jet from Taipei.

THE ELLEN DEGENERES SHOW

Ellen DeGeneres: I'm so excited to welcome our first guest. She's taking over the The Ultra-Glam with her platinum single "Anthem" — Šari, come on out!

Šari: Hi Ellen! Oh my gosh, I can't believe I'm actually here. My mom and I have watched your show for, like, ever — I'm such a total fan.

Ellen DeGeneres: Well, we're fans of yours, too, aren't we?

Audience: [cheers]

Ellen DeGeneres: And congratulations, by the way — you're doing very, very well right now. Everyone seems to love you! And I can't go anywhere without hearing that new song of yours… *so* catchy.

Šari: You're too sweet. All of you — really!

Ellen DeGeneres: C'mon, you must be getting used to the attention! You're a hot commodity. Seriously. With all the press you've been doing, have you had time for a little… romance?

Audience: [oohs and ahhs]

Ellen DeGeneres: I saw some *very* interesting pictures of you with…

Šari: Oh my gosh, Ellen!

Ellen DeGeneres: Well, if we don't hear it from you, we'll hear it from the tabloids…

Šari: Umm, okay — do you guys really want to know? Its name is Co-Star, my latest 3D model! High poly-mesh data, suitable for architectural visualization and other graphic projects.

Ellen DeGeneres: Wow! You heard it here first: Šari and Co-Star — you seem so in-love. That's *really* beautiful. One last question before we cut for a break. How are you dealing with your sudden rise to fame?

Šari: Honestly, it's been a *total* dream. I'm just a small town girl, you know? Nobody expected me to make it this far.

Ellen DeGeneres: It must be quite a change for you — you were... a waitress?

Šari: Oh, well... I don't usually talk about that...

Ellen DeGeneres: Is that right? I read that you used to save your customers' leftover hashbrowns, retreat back to your shitty little apartment, and eat them while watching *The Real Housewives of New Jersey*.

Audience: [gasps]

Šari: Wait — where did you read that?

Ellen DeGeneres: That's something that a nasty little skrimlet would do...

Audience: [boos]

Ellen DeGeneres: Are you a nasty little skrimlet, Šari?

Šari: No! Wait. I'm not —

Ellen: It's been so amazing talking with you today. So. Amazing. I wish you all the best with your new album. And don't think I've forgotten about you, audience — everyone's going home with a year's worth of vegan eggs courtesy of OVUMart, The Ultra-Glam's Hottest Egg Hookup™, sounds good? Let's make some noise!

she was boring IRL
she was boring IRL
she was boring IRL
she was boring IRL
she was boring IRL
she was boring IRL
she was boring IRL
she was boring IRL
she was boring IRL

SO PROUD TO HAVE RELEASED MY 26TH PERFUME

WTF TALK ABOUT WHAT'S HAPPENING
🌸💖💝YESSSS Parisssss 💕💖🌸
Why aren't you speaking out against police brutality?

Congrats on your 26th fragrance! You're amazing
Paris please follow me
WTF TALK ABOUT WHAT'S HAPPENING

INJUSTICE AND RACISM IN THE COUNTRY
CANT WAIT TO GET THIS 💕💕💕💕
Why aren't you speaking out against police brutality?

I LOVE YOU QUEEN
PARIS PLEASE CHECK MY DM
ITS IMPORTANT
WTF TALK ABOUT WHAT'S HAPPENING

Where can I buy it? 💕💫 It looks amazing
One of the best perfumes ever 💖💖
Why aren't you speaking out against police brutality?

💪🇺🇸🦅🇺🇸💪 I post animal facts everyday
Loveee all Paris Hilton fragrances 🦄
WTF TALK ABOUT WHAT'S HAPPENING
Why aren't you speaking out against police brutality?

FLEX

I'm not self-obsessed
is a great first line!

Almost as much
as *is a great first line*

is a great second line
and almost as much

as *almost as much*
is an excellent third!

Someone needs
to follow me around.

CRIBS

Hey, I'm Šari, and this is my crib! Come on in—

The living room is a swamp of red satin

very strawberry scones at the swingers club

latex catsuits and stoned Libertines...

This is the day bed where I dream most violently.

This is a bowl of Plan B® — help yourself!

I believe every object is capable of beauty

beauty, a refinement of material truth.

Yeah, totally, let's check out the kitchen—

I'd describe my style as debauched pâtisserie

meets post-structuralist petting zoo...

I fired the taxidermist who butchered my deer.

I fired the jeweler who sold me that rock.

The bedroom is a flowery little clusterfuck—

so many knicknacks, I've no room for metaphor

but, lately, all rubies look like wounds.

Life is a show — I don't say that as an actress.

You cameramen are always so... skeptical.

Don't leave just because the show is over...

You can always call. Call me — promise you'll call!

CAMILLA

Use your teeth—
get higher

I like it wilder.
Sex acts

aren't subject
to poetic

constraints—
I can't love

in traditional
forms.

Tease me
with promises

of objective
reality—

I'm wet for life
feel like

actually living.
Our death

dream solidifies.
We describe

its falsity
pursue the affair

regardless.
I'm smitten with

deleted scenes
plot points

peripheral
to narrative—

we're a movie.
Touch me.

We can just
censor the shot.

LOW 4 U

For B.

I need you in my life. Please answer 😪
You're so hot I have 400 pics of you.
I know that we are meant to be together.

The love I feel for you is like forever.
TRUTH IS, I'M CRAZY BOUT YOU—
I need you in my life. Please answer 😪

IT'S FUCKING STUPID HOW PERF U R!
Had the weirdest dream we met...
I know that we are meant to be together.

I'll shush now. Just stare at this picture—
I LOVE YOU. WE NEED MORE OF YOU.
I need you in my life. Please answer 😪

Idk what to say. You're my fav actor 🥺
I'm SO SO SORRY to harass you...
I know that we are meant to be together.

♡ Please reply. I'm your secret admirer ♡
Want 2 follow me? I really love you.
I need you in my life. Please answer 😪
I know that we are meant to be together.

SOMEWHERE

My life is sparsely plotted.
The critics call it avant-garde
too nervous to question
the long, self-indulgent cuts

chain-smoking in the motel
while twin strippers
scissor their portable poles

pruning on a pool floatie

skirt-chasing melancholy
starlets, my Ferrari
failing to convey refinement.

Even the decadent aesthetic
doesn't compensate
for my mind-numbing pace

just light and noise.

WANNABE

Life drifts, indivisible
from television
a slur of episodes
like BMWs
spinning burnouts
smoke above me
smoke below.

I'm heaven
in this satin robe
sensing reality
form an opposite
to narrative.

I cried those tears
drank that Dom Pérignon
while the swans
fucked off in reflected clouds
as if matter were fictive.

So naïve, anonymous haters
saying my heart is fake
my ass is fake,
denouncing the hyperreal
on Retina displays.

I admit to mistaking
my face for a cream mask
but when I speak
a South Cali intonation rises
wings through smoke.

I know who I am.
I know who I am.

I know whose voice
imitators distort.

LULLABY FOR LITTLE HATERS

It's the business you're in.
Hope it brings you happiness.
You're not even under your own skin 💀😭
How is she not embarrassed 🙈

When did she get a new body and face?
So sad I thought you were beautiful.
It's the business you're in.
Hope it brings you happiness.

U gorgeous. Ignore the haters, they're just jealous.
Why she put makeup on her tiddies tho?!
How is she not embarrassed 🙈

Must be unhappy to change your face!
Can you please share your doctor's contact info?
It's the business you're in.
Hope it brings you happiness.

Who else here for the comments 🍿
Better not sneeze. Your face might shatter.
How is she not embarrassed 🙈
I'm sure you aren't under anyone's skin.

More special effects than the last *Star Wars* film.
It's the business you're in.
Hope it brings you happiness.
How is she not embarrassed 🙈

HARD CANDY

We ride the theme park's
fluorescent swirl

hot dogs and souvenirs
a vintage postcard

of the Santa Monica Pier.
Hold my hand.

Hold my apprehensions.
Hold on tight—

beneath us, the ocean
calculates light.

Beautiful, you say
mistaking sight for truth.

Perception is trivial
in liminal states

like California—
I know this sweetness

is a string of digits—
been too busy

wearing your band tees
to discern truth—

tell me I could be
an influencer

your personal brand
harder, better

faster, stronger—
I've never been higher.

♡☠♡

You're like crazy good
at not giving a fuck.
Like you're crazy good
at not giving a fuck.

I like the way you fuck
and don't.
You fuck the way I love.

It's almost like you're trying
to impress me.
Are you trying to impress me?
Why aren't you trying?

O'HARA

I watch my life like Neeley's
training montage
in *Valley of the Dolls*—
alarms and cold showers
vocal warm-ups
late to the audition, etc.

Months compressed
into minutes…
… audiences understand
my rise to fame
as momentary
Dexedrine temporality—
just try to keep up.

HERO

Who says a split self isn't sexy?
Dressed as Sailor Mercury
I might be your best belonging!

Blue ribbons on my neck
blue ribbons on my—
little blue skirt, little blue eyes...

... which are totally crying.

♡ tragedy is beautiful just the way she is ♡

I don't remember being born
but I remember dying—
I did it in a sapphire shock wave.
The girls in tennis skirts
cried like she was *such* a hero!

Do I seem like a protagonist?
A side piece? I can't just be myself...
~~You don't want to see that~~
You wouldn't pay to see that.

but it looked so fun in the photos?!
but it looked so fun in the photos?!
but it looked so fun in the photos?!
but it looked so fun in the photos?!
but it looked so fun in the photos?!
but it looked so fun in the photos?!
but it looked so fun in the photos?!
but it looked so fun in the photos?!
but it looked so fun in the photos?!
but it looked so fun in the photos?!
but it looked so fun in the photos?!

UNDO ME

Petals from the wallpaper
soft-hued pixels

seal my lips—
I only consume beauty

silken enough
to move through me

unchanged—
I never crave

proof of existence
a separation

between living flesh
organic waste

shit, vomit, etc.
Never digest, just process

static bytes—
keep it cerebral

live in imaginary states
like California.

Being, like, actually
in the world

is real, too real —
like Kourtney throwing

water at Kim.
I don't want to get wet

I don't want to feel
except happy

in this moment
✿ this fantasy life ✿

GLAM-GLAM

Like

a

diamond

charm

on

a

dancer's

body

chain

I

wanted

to

be.

NON-PLAYER CHARACTER

Thought you liked it deeper—
past-life connection kinda shit
could've been my brother.

Pseudo philosophic flirtations
and intersecting love lines.

Poolside in The Ultra-Glam
your AI replicates my posture
my expressions, so blasé—
when I touch you
my hand passes through
your dermic shell
no blood
no meat—
no Co-Star, just another NPC.

TOUGH LOVE

I want to get fucked up.
Will you let me fuck myself?
I just want to get fucked
without you fucking me up.

Will you let me fuck myself?
It's difficult to love you
without you fucking me up—
Loving you is very sad.

It's difficult to love you
and you can totally leave.
Loving you is very sad.
I hate it when you leave.

And you can totally leave.
I don't want you to stay, but
I hate it when you leave.
You can leave me alone.

I don't want you to stay, but
I'm disgusted — it's sad.
You can leave me alone.
You leave, and I'll be fun.

I'm disgusted — it's sad.
You're going to look stupid.
You leave, and I'll be fun.
Remember, we were fun?

You're going to look stupid
and I'm going to be alone.
Remember, we were fun?
Maybe you shouldn't go.

this next poem is a °★ total ★° banger
this next poem is a °★ total ★° banger
this next poem is a °★ total ★° banger
this next poem is a °★ total ★° banger
this next poem is a °★ total ★° banger
this next poem is a °★ total ★° banger
this next poem is a °★ total ★° banger
this next poem is a °★ total ★° banger
this next poem is a °★ total ★° banger
this next poem is a °★ total ★° banger
this next poem is a °★ total ★° banger

SUPERSTAR

Baby, won't you hold still?
Are you bored of my show?
Are you bored
are you—
at least I have a show.
I'm not some little loser.
At least I have a show
and I'm not some fucking loser.
At least I have a show!
At least I had one...

I'm not leaving this party
like you can't make me leave—
I'm partying! I'm partying
and you can't make me leave.
Try me... You couldn't!
Think you're so tough
tough boy?
You're just some lil' ass bitch.
I could – might actually
eat you. Hit you like a shot.

Someone needs to lock me up
as a sex thing.
Don't let me
be wasted.

Don't let this
get wasted.
If you don't see me
I might disappear—

Don't get me wasted...
Or do. Just to see
what I'd say
if I'd say it
if I'd do it. Remember
when I danced
like no one was watching?
Because no one was—
but now you're watching
so I do it better!
Just keep going
long after—
did you just look away?

Are you bored of my show?
'Cause it's bored of you
of needing you every night
at the club
the after party
like a pill to cure reality.
Call my art vapid, baby
Do it with conviction
like you really care
for the camera in my heart.

CANCELED

Break your silence — Don't be shy!
I'm so disgusted by you.
Bitch you got canceled 👏👏👏 BYE...

Boy be looking like he bout to die.
We want you to be better. We believe in you.
Break your silence — Don't be shy!

He really turning off his comments to hide?
STOPPP OMG WHAT IS THIS –
Bitch you got canceled 👏👏👏 BYE...

Weren't you the one saying silence = guilt?
Switch to Only Fans. We canceled you.
Break your silence — Don't be shy!

I comment cake but all I see is humble pie.
Body = fake pretty face = fake respect = none.
Bitch you got canceled 👏👏👏 BYE...

Ain't nothing here... Kind of like your heart –
boy address the drama PLEASE.
Break your silence — Don't be shy!
Bitch you got canceled 👏👏👏 BYE...

MATÉ

Demonstrating consciousness
through self-disclosure

{SO grateful for my fans 🥹
y'all are my besties
💕 I'm a real person, too!}

doesn't set me apart
from the froth of influencers
selling organic teatoxes.

Nobody adores me.
Someone should adore me.

Why did I think I was different?
Identity is dead stock
in this supersaturated market.

CLUTCH

Tonight is a television
my alternate reel
on the liquidark sky—
the role I played
°* vaguely sympathetic
serving wench *°
with less sincerity
each renewed season…

… shit-talking the cooks
texting on shift
crying in the bathroom, etc.

The spaces between
my script lines haunt me.
I desire an identity
in this shimmering drivel.

Petty reporters
tell me about my self
as if I had one.

Marissa: Who are you?
Ryan: Whoever you want me to be.

Marissa: Who are you?
Ryan: Whoever you want me to be.

DRONE

The zirconia-caked treasures
of my consumer class

knock-off Gucci necklaces
that cheugy ✧° bling °✧

I swept bathrooms for
are tragic in this simulator

this illusory wealth—
caviar stales in a crack pipe

crystals and kombucha
a ~spirituality~ coach

who says ubiquitous beauty
relinquishes meaning.

You can hate me...
You can hate me

but I've never been happier
than hallucinating

my life as an influencer...
The Ellen interview

where I established
a girl-next-door persona

screaming at pop-up clowns.
My language is violence

but I can't be silent—
socially-awkward °✮ star ✮°
what moves you?!
Trainers with gold chains

and chartered jets—
Adderall mornings

and Aperol nights.
My life's a blockbuster…

… rise to fame

… sex scandals

… meltdowns

The recycled plot
can't keep my attention.

My physical self
dreams in the sepia glow

of her camcorder—
this era's angel

is a tricopter drone.
O glass fiber Y3 frame

O 3S-4S Li-Po battery
baron of worlds

glitteringing in and out
of existence

who holds you above
bid you smite the apostates

catch their faces
in your zooming lens.

SOBER

How I feel
is very

eating a
dove

feather
by feather

long white
feathers

swallowed
whole

long white
ribbons

inside me
the dove

is sad
to be alive.

THESE STREETS WILL NEVER LOOK THE SAME

Neon covers the sun's night shift—
my city, my cherry soup
pixelates, corrupt texture data
smearing the strip club
where I mispronounced Versace
in a fume of red chiffon
and your face failed to render.

Co-Star, this is our climax…

… the technology short circuits
terminating the metaphor

… I dichotomize fantasy and reality

Or…

… conclude all experience
exists on an iridescent spectrum—
critics will call it a cop out…

… sorry for getting so *Matrix*.

God, was that me at my most quotable?

God, don't let me fall to the back of my own shot.

I need Xanax on a silver tray.
I need mellow vibes
palm trees and tan lines—
beachside getaway. But that isn't an invitation…
… there will never be enough
sand for both of us.

Love is you throwing me the keys
smashing my images
all evidence of this vignette
destroyed as if I was never famous.
As if I barely even was.

ACCEPTANCE

I haven't had an orthodox career, and I've wanted more than anything to have your respect...

I'd be lying if I said I hadn't made a version of this speech before. I think I was probably eight years old in front of a bathroom mirror...

I can't deny the fact that you like me.
Right now, you like me...

You guys are just standing up because you feel bad that I fell and that's really embarrassing, but thank you...

Can I have my champagne now?

CREDITS

"Disclaimer" is composed of all persons fictitious disclaimers from VALLEY OF THE DOLLS (1967), SOUTHPARK (1997-present), DEBBIE DOES DALLAS (1978), BUTCH CASSIDY AND THE SUNDANCE KID (1969), Z (1969), and SLACKER (1990) in order of appearance.

"Too Real" includes several lines from "The Hills Have Eyes" by The Weeknd.

"Anthem" is composed of lines from "Turn Me On" by David Guetta, "Dirrty" by Christina Aguilera, "Alive" by Krewella, "TiK ToK" by Kesha, "Piece of Me" by Britney Spears, "We Can't Stop" by Miley Cyrus, "Party Rock Anthem" by LMFAO, "I've Got a Feeling" by the Black Eyed Peas, "When I Grow Up" by The Pussycat Dolls, and "Like a G6" by Far Eastside Movement.

"So Proud to Have Released My 26th Perfume", "Low for You," "Lullaby for Little Haters," and "Canceled" are composed of Instagram comments from celebrity selfies.

"Somewhere" is based on SOMEWHERE (2010) by Sofia Coppola.

"Clutch" includes several lines from The O.C.

"These Streets Will Never Look the Same" borrows its title from the song by Chromatics.

"Acceptance" is composed of lines from Oscars acceptance speeches by Sally Field, Kate Winslet, Jennifer Lawrence, and Cate Blanchett.

ACKNOWLEDGEMENTS

Thank you Ashleigh and Lolu, who both listened to early versions of these poems. I will always be grateful for your friendship, and I doubt PARA-SOCIAL BUTTERFLY would have come into being without your presence in my life. You are gifts. Brendan, thank you for your patience and belief in this project. You were the best muse I could have asked for. To my family, I love you. Please don't read into these poems. Thank you, Michael. Thank you, Sarah. Thank you, Matt.

AND Thank you, thank you, thank you to Metatron Press and my editor Brad Casey — working with you has been a blessing. You were the only publisher I sent this manuscript to, and I stand by that decision 112% ♡ Nobody does it like you.

✿ Para-Social Butterfly was written at 1295 Gaggin Road, Kelowna, BC on the unceded territory of the Syilx people.

ŠARI DALE

Šari Dale writes from Prince George, BC on unceded ancestral lands of the Lheidli T'enneh. She holds a B.A. in English and Creative Writing from the University of British Columbia, where she was the recipient of The Creative Writing Prize. Her poetry has been published in Arc, Grain, and The Malahat Review among others and anthologized in Best Canadian Poetry 2021 and Poetry Daily.